Peanut Butter and Chocolate Recipe Heaven Volume 1

By Tiffany Barrett

United States

Peanut Butter and Chocolate Recipe Heaven Volume 1

By Tiffany Barrett

© 2013 Tiffany Barrett, All rights reserved.

No part of this publication may be reproduced or transmitted in any form or by any means, mechanical or electronic, including photocopying and recording, or by any informational storage or retrieval system, without permission in writing from author or publisher (except by a reviewer, who may quote brief passages and/or show brief video clips in a review).

Disclaimer: The Publisher and the Author make no representation or warranties with respect to the accuracy or completeness of the contents of this work and specifically disclaim all warranties, including without limitation, warranties of fitness for a particular purpose. No warranty may be created or extended by sales or promotional materials. The advice and strategies contained herein may not be suitable for every situation. This work is sold with the understanding that the Publisher is not engaged in rendering legal, accounting, or other professional services. If professional assistance is required, the services of a competent professional person should be sought. Neither the Publisher nor the Author shall be liable for damages arising herefrom. The fact that an organization or website is referred to in this work as a citation and/or a potential source of further information does not mean that the Author or the Publisher endorses the information the organization or website may provide or recommendations it may make. Further, readers should be aware that internet websites listed in this work may have changed or disappeared between the time this work was written and when it is read.

ISBN-13: 978-1481994903

ISBN-10: 1481994905

Printed in the United States of America

This book is dedicated to
everyone who lives for chocolate and peanut butter …
I share your passion.

Acknowledgements

A special thanks to Megan Kellett of CookingWhims.com for the cover photo, Chocolate Peanut Butter Torte. Visit Megan's website for many more excellent and decadent recipes. If your mouth is already watering to make it, jump to page 22 to go right to the recipe.

Before You Get Started ...

I know you're anxious to get to the recipes and create a mouth-watering memory but I wanted to explain something first. I'll make it quick, I promise.

This is not your typical book with each new item beginning on the right-hand page. But let me explain and it will become abundantly clear. ☺

Some of the recipes in this book – OK, LOTS of the recipes in this book – have many steps and involve quite a few ingredients. So rather than make you turn the page to see all the ingredients, I opted to start each recipe on the left-hand page so that in case the ingredients spilled over (pun intended) onto the second page, you would still be able to see all of them before getting into the instruction section.

Just one more thing … the recipes in this book will not help you lose weight but we all know that. So enjoy making and eating them and avoid the scales for a few days afterwards. ☺

Thanks and happy peanut-butter-and-chocolating!

Tiff

Table of Contents

Acknowledgements i

Before You Get Started …... ii

Mega Peanut Butter Cups 6

Peanut Butter Chocolate Brownies 8

Peanut Butter Chocolate Delight...10

Chocolate Peanut Butter Swirled Cheesecake 12

Chocolate Peanut Butter Rice Krispie® Bars 16

Chocolate Peanut Butter Sandwiches 20

Chocolate Peanut Butter Torte 22

Macaroni Grill® Reese's® Peanut Butter Cake 24

Peanut Butter Chocolate Brownies 26

Chocolate Peanut Butter Banana Bread 28

Chocolate Peanut Butter Pretzel Cupcakes..............................30

Chocolate Peanut Butter Squares..34

Crispy Chocolate Peanut Butter French Toast..........................36

Peanut Butter Truffle Brownies 38

Chocolate Peanut Butter Cupcakes 40

Red Robin Mountain High Mudd Pie® 44

Chocolate Peanut Butter Chip Cookies.....................................48

Chocolate Peanut Butter Cream Cheesecake 50

Peanut Butter Chocolate Chip Pound Cake 52

Peanut Butter and Chocolate Biscotti 54

Mrs. Fields Peanut Butter Dream Bars® 56

Chocolate PBC Ice Cream 58

Chocolate Peanut Butter Cake 60

Chocolate Peanut Butter Cream Pie...62

Chocolate Peanut Butter Bark...64

v

Mega Peanut Butter Cups

Ingredients

2 cups (16 ounces) semi-sweet or milk chocolate chips
2 Tablespoons unsalted butter, room temperature
1/3 cup powdered sugar
1/2 cup creamy peanut butter

Instructions

Microwave half of the chocolate chips in a small glass microwave safe bowl for 30-60 seconds.

Remove from the microwave when the chips begin to melt.

Stir with a fork until smooth.

The heat of the chocolate will melt the remaining chips.

If necessary, reheat in 10 second intervals until smooth.

Be careful not to scorch the chocolate.

Fill muffin tin with cupcake papers.

Spoon about 2 teaspoons of melted chocolate into the bottom of each cup.

Tap the pan on the counter to smooth and spread the chocolate evenly.

Place the muffin pan in the freezer for about 15 minutes to harden.

While the chocolate hardens, prepare the peanut butter layer.

In a small bowl, mix peanut butter, butter and powdered sugar until smooth.

Remove the pan from the freezer.

Spread a small amount of peanut butter over the chocolate layer.

Tap on counter again to smooth and spread the peanut butter.

Return the muffin pan to the freezer for 15 more minutes to harden.

Melt the remaining chocolate in the same manner, being careful not to scorch.

Remove muffin pan from freezer and spread the final chocolate layer over the peanut butter.

Return to freezer until ready to serve.

Serve cold.

Peanut Butter Chocolate Brownies

Ingredients

2 ounces unsweetened chocolate
¼ cup butter or margarine, room temperature
¼ cup creamy peanut butter
1 cup packed light brown sugar
2 large eggs
1 teaspoon vanilla
½ cup sifted all-purpose flour
¾ cup chopped unsalted roasted peanuts

Instructions

Preheat oven to 325 ° F.

In a small bowl, melt chocolate in microwave for 30-60 seconds, checking occasionally to ensure it does not scorch.

In a large bowl, cream butter, peanut butter and sugar until light and fluffy.

Add eggs one at a time, beating well after each addition.

Add vanilla and melted chocolate.

Fold in flour and ½ cup peanuts.

Pour into greased 8 x 8" pan.

Sprinkle with remaining peanuts.

Bake for 30-35 minutes or until edges just begin to pull away from sides of pan.

Cool completely in the pan on a wire rack before cutting into 16 brownies.

Makes 16 brownies

Peanut Butter Chocolate Delight

Ingredients

20 Oreo® cookies, divided
2 Tablespoons butter, softened
1 (8 ounce) package cream cheese, softened
1/2 cup peanut butter
1-1/2 cups powdered sugar, divided
1 (16-ounce) carton Cool Whip, thawed and divided
15 miniature peanut butter cups, chopped
1 cup cold milk
1 (3.9-ounce) package instant chocolate fudge pudding mix

Instructions

Using a food processor, crush 16 Oreos® and combine with butter.

Press into an ungreased 9" square pan.

In a large bowl, combine the cream cheese, peanut butter and 1 cup powdered sugar, beating until smooth.

Fold in half of the Cool Whip.

Spread cream cheese mixture over crust.

Spread with chopped peanut butter cups.

In another medium bowl, combine the milk, pudding mix and remaining powdered sugar and blend thoroughly.

Let stand until soft-set, about 2 minutes.

Fold in the remaining Cool Whip.

Spread over peanut butter cups.

Crush remaining Oreos® and sprinkle over the top.

Cover and refrigerate for at least 3 hours before serving.

Makes 12-16 servings

11

Chocolate Peanut Butter Swirled Cheesecake

Ingredients

Crust
1-1/2 cups chocolate graham cracker crumbs
6 Tablespoons sugar
6 Tablespoons butter, melted

Filling
½ cup (4 ounces) semisweet chocolate
1/2 cup smooth peanut butter
¼ cup light corn syrup
4 (8-ounce) packages cream cheese, room temperature
1-3/4 cups sugar
1 cup heavy whipping cream, divided
4 eggs, lightly beaten
2 teaspoons vanilla

Topping
1 cup (8 ounces) semisweet chocolate, finely chopped
1 cup heavy cream
Reese's® peanut butter cups, coarsely chopped
1/4 cup peanuts, coarsely chopped

Instructions

Preheat oven to 325 ° F.

Crust

In a medium bowl, thoroughly mix graham cracker crumbs, sugar and melted butter.

Press into the bottom of a greased 10" springform pan.

Place pan on cookie sheet and bake for 10 minutes.

Cool on a wire rack.

Filling

In a microwave safe bowl, place the semisweet chocolate, peanut butter, and corn syrup.

Microwave for 30-60 seconds or until the chocolate is melted.

Remove the chocolate mixture just before completely melted and stir to complete the melting. This prevents it from scorching.

Stir until smooth.

Add 1/4 cup of heavy cream and mix well to combine.
In a large bowl, beat cream cheese and sugar until smooth.

Gradually mix in the remaining 3/4 cup of the cream.

Add eggs and vanilla and beat just until combined.
Pour half of the filling into the cooled crust.

Spoon half of the chocolate / peanut butter mixture over the filling.

Gently swirl the chocolate / peanut butter mixture into the filling using a small spatula or butter knife.

Top with the remaining filling and chocolate / peanut butter mixture.

Repeat the swirling.
Place cheesecake back on the cookie sheet.

Bake for 70-75 minutes or until center is almost set.
Place on a wire rack and cool for 10 minutes.

Carefully run a knife around inside edge of pan to loosen.

Cool cheesecake completely before covering with plastic wrap and refrigerating overnight.

The next day remove the springform pan (sides only) and place cheesecake, including pan bottom on serving platter or cake plate.

In a small bowl, place chopped chocolate.

Bring cream to a boil in a small saucepan.

Pour boiling cream over chocolate and blend until smooth.

Cool slightly and pour over cheesecake.

Garnish top with chopped peanut butter cups and peanuts.
Refrigerate about 1 hour or until topping is set.
Store in refrigerator.

15

Chocolate Peanut Butter Rice Krispie® Bars

NOTE: This recipe requires a candy thermometer.

Ingredients

Bottom layer
3 1/2 cups Rice Krispies®
1/2 cup water
1/2 cup granulated sugar
6 Tablespoons light corn syrup
6 Tablespoons unsalted butter, melted

Middle layer
7 1/2 ounces milk chocolate, chopped
1 1/2 cups creamy peanut butter

Top layer
6 ounces good quality dark chocolate, chopped
1 teaspoon light corn syrup
½ cup unsalted butter

Bottom Layer
Line a 9x13" baking pan with parchment paper leaving excess hanging over the side for easy removal.

Instructions

Place the Rice Krispies® in a large bowl and set aside.

In a medium saucepan, mix 1/2 cup water; sugar and corn syrup.

Place a candy thermometer in the sugar mixture and bring to a boil over medium-high heat.

Cook until the candy thermometer reaches 235° F, the soft-ball stage.

Remove from heat and add butter.

Pour the sugar mixture over the Rice Krispies®.

Working quickly, blend until the cereal is thoroughly coated.

Pour the mixture into the prepared pan.

Press the mixture evenly into the bottom of the pan, using a spatula coated with non-stick cooking spray.

Cool the layer to room temperature.

Middle Layer

In a large microwave safe bowl, combine the chocolate and peanut butter.

Microwave on high for 60-90 seconds, checking every 15 seconds to ensure the mixture doesn't scorch.

If more time is needed, microwave in 10-second burst until mixture is smooth.

Continue to stir for about 30 seconds to cool the mixture slightly.

Pour over the cooled crust.

Place the pan in the refrigerator for about 1 hour or until the top layer hardens.

Top Layer

In another large microwave safe bowl, combine the dark chocolate, corn syrup and butter.

Microwave on high for 60-90 seconds, checking every 15 seconds to ensure the mixture doesn't scorch.

If more time is needed, microwave in 10-second burst until mixture is smooth.

Continue to stir for about 30 seconds to cool the mixture slightly.

Pour the dark chocolate mixture over the chilled peanut butter layer and spread until smooth.

Chill for about 1 hour or until the chocolate layer hardens. Using the parchment overhang, carefully lift the bars from the pan.

Cut into squares and serve cold.

Covered tightly, the bars can be stored in the refrigerator for up to 4 days.

Makes 24 2" squares

19

Chocolate Peanut Butter Sandwiches

Ingredients

3 cups good quality chopped milk chocolate
4 Tablespoons butter
12 graham crackers, halved
2 cups creamy peanut butter

Instructions

Combine chocolate and butter in a microwave safe bowl.

Microwave on high for 60-90 seconds, or just until almost melted.

Stir to complete the melting.

If more time is needed, microwave in 10-second burst until mixture is smooth.

Be careful not to scorch.

Dip and coat each graham cracker in chocolate and let harden on wax or parchment paper.

Place in the freezer for a few minutes to speed this up.

Spread 2 Tablespoons of peanut butter over each dipped graham cracker.

Place the graham crackers in the freezer for 10 more minutes.

Important! While the peanut butter is hardening in the freezer, stir the remaining chocolate to make sure it is of spreading consistency but not too liquid. If need be, return it to the microwave for just enough time to melt it slightly.

Carefully spoon melted chocolate over the tops and sides of the peanut butter.

Slowly use a small spoon to work the chocolate around the edges and sides.

A small plastic knife can help to smooth the chocolate around the edges.

Return to the freezer for another 10 minutes to completely harden.

Serve chilled; they melt fast once you begin to handle them.

Makes 12 sandwiches

Chocolate Peanut Butter Torte

Ingredients

Brownie Layers:
1 cup butter, melted
1 cup cocoa powder
2 cups sugar
4 eggs
1 Tablespoons vanilla
1 cup flour
1/2 teaspoon salt
15 mini Reese's peanut butter cups, chopped
Filling:
1/4 cup peanut butter, warmed for easy spreading
Peanut Butter Ganache
3 Tablespoons peanut butter
1/2 cup heavy cream
1/4 cup powdered sugar (plus more if needed for desired consistency)
1/2 teaspoon vanilla
Chocolate chips and chopped peanut butter cups for decoration

Instructions

Brownie layers

Preheat oven to 350 ° F.

Butter two 8-inch round pans, lining the bottoms with parchment paper.

In a large mixing bowl, combine the melted butter and cocoa until cocoa is dissolved.

Add sugar, 1/4 cup at a time, mixing well after each addition.

Add eggs one at a time, beating well after each addition.

Add vanilla, flour, and salt and mix only until the flour is no longer visible.

Gently fold in chopped peanut butter cups and distribute batter evenly between the two pans.

Bake for 25 minutes or until a toothpick inserted in center comes out clean.

Allow to cool on a wire rack.

When the layers are cool to the touch, place one layer on a cake plate.

Filling

Using a microwave safe bowl, warm the peanut butter in the microwave for 20-30 seconds, or until of spreading consistency.

Spread the peanut butter over the bottom layer.

Place the second brownie layer on top of the peanut butter filling.

Peanut Butter Ganache

In a small bowl, thoroughly blend 3 Tablespoons peanut butter, powdered sugar, vanilla, and cream.

If the ganache is too thin, add a little more powdered sugar until it reaches the desired consistency.

Pour the glaze over the cake, allowing it to drip down the sides.

Garnish with chocolate chips and / or chopped peanut butter cups as desired.

Refrigerate leftovers.

Macaroni Grill®
Reese's® Peanut Butter Cake

Ingredients

Cake
¾ cup (1 ½ sticks) butter, softened
¾ cup creamy peanut butter
2 cups packed light brown sugar
3 eggs
2 cups all-purpose flour
1 Tablespoon baking powder
½ teaspoon salt
1 cup milk
1 teaspoon vanilla

Peanut Butter Filling
1 (8-ounce) package cream cheese, softened
½ cup creamy peanut butter

Chocolate Glaze
½ cup water
¼ cup (1/2 stick) butter
½ cup cocoa powder
1 cup powdered sugar
1 teaspoon vanilla

Instructions

Preheat oven to 350 º F.

Grease and flour two 9-inch round cake pans.

In a large bowl, cream the butter and peanut butter until fluffy.

Add brown sugar and mix thoroughly.

Add eggs, one at a time, blending well after each addition.

In a small bowl, combine flour, baking powder, and salt.

Add the flour mixture and milk to the butter mixture alternately, ending with flour and blend thoroughly.

Add vanilla.

Pour into prepared pans.

Bake for 45 minutes or until a toothpick inserted in the center of each cake comes out clean.

After the cake has cooled for 5 minutes, turn out on a wire rack to cool.

Gently remove the pan from the cake, allowing it to cool completely before frosting.

Peanut butter filling

Cream the peanut butter and cream cheese together until fluffy.

Spread half of the peanut butter filling over the top of each cake.

Let chill in the refrigerator.

Chocolate glaze

Combine butter and water in a small saucepan and bring to a boil.

Stir in cocoa, confectioner's sugar, and vanilla and mix until smooth.

Using a metal spatula dipped in hot water, frost each cake with the chocolate glaze. It will harden as it cools.

Makes 2 9-inch cakes

Peanut Butter Chocolate Brownies

Ingredients

Brownie Layer
1 ½ sticks (3/4 cup) unsalted butter
1 cup semisweet chocolate chips
1 1/4 cups sugar
1 1/2 teaspoons vanilla extract
1/4 teaspoon kosher salt
4 large eggs
1 cup all-purpose flour
3/4 cup roasted salted peanuts, coarsely chopped

Peanut Butter Layer
1 cup peanut butter (not natural or old-fashioned)
½ stick (1/4 cup) unsalted butter, room temperature
1 cup powdered sugar
3 Tablespoons whole milk
1 teaspoon vanilla extract

Chocolate Frosting
1/4 cup unsalted butter, softened
1/4 cup cocoa powder, sifted
1/2 teaspoon vanilla extract
1 cup powdered sugar
2 Tablespoons whole milk

Topping
1 cup Peanut Butter Cups, cut into quarters
Brownies

Instructions

Preheat oven to 350 ° F.

Line a 9 X 9" pan with foil, allowing the foil to extend about 2" above either side of the pan.

Butter the foil or coat with non-stick cooking spray.

In a large bowl, microwave the butter and chocolate for 60-90 seconds or until chocolate begins to melt.

Be careful not to scorch.

Remove from microwave and stir with a fork to finish melting.

Beat in the sugar until thoroughly blended.

Add eggs, vanilla extract and kosher salt.

Gradually stir in the flour until thoroughly blended.

Add the salted peanuts and stir just until well distributed.

Spread the batter in pan and bake for 22-25 minutes or until toothpick inserted in center comes out with moist crumbs attached.

Be careful not to overbake.

Allow the brownies to cool to room temperature.

Peanut Butter Layer

Using an electric mixer, combine the peanut butter and 1/4 cup softened unsalted butter in medium bowl and blend until smooth.

Add the powdered sugar, milk and vanilla.

The mixture should be of spreading consistency. If, for some odd reason, it isn't, add a little more milk.

Smoothly spread the peanut butter layer over the cool brownies.

Refrigerate the brownies while making the chocolate frosting.

Chocolate Frosting

Beat all the ingredients together in a medium-sized bowl.

When the mixture looks like frosting, spread over the peanut butter layer.

Sprinkle with quartered Peanut Butter Cups.

Cut into squares.

Makes 12-16 brownies

Chocolate Peanut Butter Banana Bread

Ingredients

½ cup butter, room temperature
½ cup peanut butter
1/3 cup brown sugar
1/3 cup sugar
1 egg
1 teaspoon vanilla extract
4-5 large ripe bananas, mashed
2 cups all-purpose flour
1/3 cup cocoa powder
1 1/4 teaspoons baking powder
1/4 teaspoon salt
1/4 teaspoon cinnamon
1/2 cup milk
1 cup chocolate chips

Instructions

Preheat oven to 350 ° F.

In a medium bowl, stir together flour, baking powder, cocoa, cinnamon and salt and set aside.

In a large bowl, cream butter and peanut butter.

Add sugars and beat about 3 minutes or until fluffy.

Add egg, vanilla and bananas, mixing thoroughly.

Slowly add dry ingredients, mixing only until combined.

Stir in milk, 1 Tablespoon at a time.

Fold in the chocolate chips.

Pour into a greased loaf pan.

Bake for 50 minutes or until toothpick inserted in center comes out clean.

Makes one loaf

29

Chocolate Peanut Butter Pretzel Cupcakes

Ingredients

Cupcakes
9 Tablespoons unsweetened cocoa powder
1 1/2 cups cake flour (not self-rising)
1/2 teaspoon salt
1 teaspoon baking soda
1/4 teaspoon baking powder
1 stick (1/2 cup) unsalted butter, softened
1 1/2 cups granulated sugar
2 large eggs, room temperature
1/2 cup strong coffee, cooled
1/2 cup whole or low-fat milk

Filling
1 cup peanut butter
1/4 cup unsalted butter, room temperature
1/4 teaspoon salt
1/2 teaspoon vanilla
2 cups powdered sugar
2 large (1/2 cup) chocolate covered pretzels, crushed

Frosting
1/2 cup butter
2/3 cup unsweetened cocoa
3 cups powdered sugar
1/3 cup milk
1 teaspoon vanilla

Garnish
package of mini chocolate covered pretzels
2-4 large chocolate covered pretzels, crushed, to sprinkle over frosting

Instructions

Preheat oven to 350 ° F.

Place oven rack in the center of the oven.

Place paper liners in two muffin pans.

In a medium bowl, sift together the cocoa, cake flour, salt, baking soda and baking powder.

Beat butter and sugar until it becomes creamy.

Add eggs one at a time, beating well after each.

Add half of the dry ingredients to the butter mixture.

In a small bowl, combine the coffee and milk.

Add the coffee and milk to the butter mixture.

Add the remainder of the dry ingredients.

Pour the batter into the muffin cups, filling them about 2/3 full.

Bake for 19-21 minutes or until a toothpick inserted in the center comes out clean.

Allow cupcakes to cool in the pan 5 minutes, then transfer to a wire rack.

Filling

Using a microwave safe bowl, combine the peanut butter, unsalted butter and salt.

Microwave on high for 30-60 seconds.

Check frequently to stir and avoid scorching.

Add powdered sugar and vanilla.

While mixture is still warm, add the crushed chocolate covered pretzels.

Using a sharp edged spoon or a melon baller, scoop out the center of each cupcake, setting aside each removed top.

Place a spoonful of filling into each indention and replace the top.

(A frosting tip is not a good tool for this because the pretzels clog the tip.)

Filling leaks are not a problem since you will be frosting the cupcakes.

Frosting

Place the butter in a medium microwave safe bowl and microwave on high for 30 seconds.

Stir in cocoa.

Alternately add powdered sugar and milk, mixing thoroughly.

Add vanilla and beat until the frosting is of spreading consistency.

Frost the cupcakes and sprinkle with the remaining crushed chocolate-covered pretzels.

Makes 18 cupcakes

33

Chocolate Peanut Butter Squares

Ingredients

Crust
22 Nabisco FAMOUS Chocolate Wafers, finely crushed (about 1⅔ cups crumbs)
¼ cup sugar
3 Tablespoons unsalted butter, softened

Filling
6 firmly packed Tablespoons dark brown sugar
2 cups powdered sugar
6 Tablespoons unsalted butter, softened
1⅓ cups creamy peanut butter
Pinch of salt
Milk Chocolate Ganache Topping
1 (11.5-ounce) bag Ghirardelli (or similar best quality) milk chocolate chips
6 Tablespoons heavy cream

Instructions

Preheat oven to 375 ° F.

Coat a 9-inch square baking pan with non-stick cooking spray.

Crust:

Mix chocolate wafers, sugar, and butter in food processor.

Using a blade attachment, pulse until cookies are finely crushed.

Press the mixture into a prepared baking pan (using your hands first, and then the bottom of a measuring cup to level it out).

Bake for 8 minutes.

Set on cooling rack till completely cooled.

While the wafer mixture is cooling, begin making the peanut butter filling.

Peanut Butter Mixture:

Mix all ingredients in a mixing bowl using a paddle attachment.

Mix (do not whip) at the lowest speed until just combined.

Refrigerate peanut butter mixture until needed.

Chocolate Ganache Topping:

Melt together milk chocolate chips and heavy cream in a microwave safe bowl on medium (50%) power for 1 to 1-1/2 minutes.

Heat at 15-30 second intervals, and stir until smooth and melted.

Do not overheat.

Finishing Steps:

Using an icing spatula, spread 1/4 cup of chocolate ganache over cooled crust.

Place in freezer to set chocolate, about 5-10 minutes.

Keep ganache smooth by stirring.

Spread peanut butter mixture over chocolate.

Spread the remaining chocolate ganache evenly over the peanut butter.

Using plastic wrap, cover pan and place in freezer for at least 1 hour or until set.

When firm, cut into small squares with a sharp knife.

This dessert is very rich!

Keep cool and serve cool.

Makes about 25 small squares

Crispy Chocolate Peanut Butter French Toast

Ingredients

4 slices thick bread
2 Tablespoons butter
3 whole eggs
1/4 cup milk
1 teaspoon vanilla
1/2 Tablespoon cinnamon
Pinch of salt
1/4 cup sugar
1 cup corn flake crumbs
1/4 cup peanut butter, melted
2 Tablespoons chocolate chips, melted

Instructions

In a large bowl, combine the eggs, milk, cinnamon, salt and vanilla.

In a shallow bowl, mix together the corn flakes and sugar.

Heat a large skillet over medium heat.

While the skillet is heating, add the bread to the egg mixture and allow to soak for about a minute.

Remove the bread from the egg mixture and dip into the cornflake mixture, making sure the bread is completely covered.

Add 1 Tablespoon of butter to the skillet.

Brown the bread in the skillet until each side is golden brown (about 2 - 3 minutes per side).

Fry the additional bread in the same way, using the remainder of the butter as needed.

Top the French toast with the melted peanut butter and chocolate chips and enjoy!

Serves 2

37

Peanut Butter Truffle Brownies

Ingredients

Brownies
1 cup butter
2 cups sugar
3 eggs
3 teaspoons vanilla
2/3 cup cocoa powder
1 cup flour
1/2 teaspoon salt
1/2 teaspoon baking powder

Peanut Butter Filling
1 stick (1/2 cup) butter, softened
1/2 cup peanut butter
2 cups powdered sugar
1-3 teaspoons milk

Ganache Topping
1/4 cup peanut butter
2 cups chocolate chips
1/4 cup butter
2 Tablespoons heavy whipping cream

Instructions

Preheat oven to 350 º F.

Butter the bottom and sides of a 9 x 13" pan.

Cover bottom of pan with parchment paper, long enough to overhang on two sides (for easy removal).

Butter the parchment paper.

Brownies

Melt butter in medium saucepan over medium heat.

Remove from heat and stir in sugar.

Add eggs and vanilla; beat until combined.

Mix in cocoa, baking powder, and salt.

Stir in flour carefully until no streaks of dry ingredients remain.

Pour mixture into the prepared baking pan and spread into an even layer.

Bake for 25 to 30 minutes.

Allow to cool completely in the pan on a cooling rack.

Filling

While the brownies cool, prepare the peanut butter filling.

Using an electric mixer, combine ingredients and beat until smooth.

Add more milk if necessary to make the mixture spreadable.

Spread into an even layer over the brownies.

Place the brownies with filling in the refrigerator for 30 minutes or until filling is set.

While the filling sets, prepare the ganache.

Ganache Topping

Mix all ingredients in a microwave safe bowl.

Melt together in microwave, checking every 15-30 seconds and stirring until evenly combined.

When the filling is set (about 30 minutes in the refrigerator), gently pour the ganache over the brownies.

Return the completed brownies to the refrigerator until set.

To serve, remove pan from refrigerator and lift out brownies using the parchment paper.

Cut brownies into squares and remove from parchment paper with a spatula.

Store in the refrigerator.

Chocolate Peanut Butter Cupcakes

Ingredients

Filling
1 cup powdered sugar
¾ cup creamy peanut butter
½ stick (1/4 cup) unsalted butter, room temperature
½ teaspoon vanilla

Cake
1 2/3 cups all-purpose flour
¾ cup unsweetened cocoa powder
1 teaspoon baking soda
½ teaspoon salt
1 cup sour cream
2 Tablespoons milk
1 teaspoon vanilla extract
1 stick (1/2 cup) unsalted butter, room temperature
1½ cups sugar
2 large eggs

Frosting
1 (8-ounce) package cream cheese, room temperature
½ stick (1/4 cup) unsalted butter, softened
½ cup creamy peanut butter
3¼ cups powdered sugar
1 cup Cool Whip

Instructions

Preheat oven to 350 ° F.

Line two cupcake pans with paper liners.

Filling

In a mixing bowl, combine powdered sugar, peanut butter, butter and vanilla.

Beat with an electric mixer on medium speed until the filling is well combined.

Roll the mixture into at least 24 1-inch sized balls.

Set these aside on a baking sheet.

Cake:

In a medium bowl, combine flour, cocoa powder, baking powder and salt.

Set aside for the moment.

In a liquid measuring cup, combine sour cream, milk and vanilla extract.

Using an electric mixer with a paddle attachment on medium-high speed, combine the butter and sugar until it is light and fluffy - about 2 minutes.

While beating, add eggs one at a time, scraping the bowl as you go.

Lower the mixer speed and add dry ingredients and sour cream mixture alternately, beginning and ending with dry ingredients.

Mix until just blended, making sure you don't overmix.

Spoon 1 - 2 Tablespoons of mixture into each cupcake liner.

Then add a peanut butter ball to each well.

Top each cupcake with the remaining cupcake mixture.

Bake for 18 - 22 minutes, or until an inserted toothpick comes out clean.

Cool for 5 - 10 minutes in the pan.

Transfer cupcakes to a wire rack until completely cool.

Frosting

Using an electric mixer, blend cream cheese, butter and peanut butter until smooth.

Slowly add powdered sugar and beat until well blended and smooth.

Add Cool Whip. The frosting should be smooth and fluffy. Frost the cooled cupcakes and decorate as desired.

Makes 24 cupcakes

43

Red Robin Mountain High Mudd Pie®

Ingredients

6 cups chocolate ice cream
1 cup peanut butter cookie pieces
6 cups vanilla ice cream
1 2/3 cups creamy peanut butter
4 chocolate flavored graham crackers
1 cup fudge topping
1 (20-ounce) squirt bottle chocolate topping
1 (20-ounce) squirt bottle caramel topping
1 can whipped cream
¾ cup chopped peanuts
12 maraschino cherries with stems

Instructions

Soften the chocolate ice cream and place in a 2 ½-3 quart mixing bowl.

Smooth the surface of the ice cream.

Sprinkle the peanut butter cookie pieces evenly over the top of the ice cream.

Cover the bowl and freeze (in the freezer) for at least one hour.

Soften the vanilla ice cream.

Remove the chocolate ice cream bowl from the freezer.

Spread the softened vanilla ice cream over the chocolate ice cream and cookie pieces.

Smooth and level the surface of the ice cream, all the way to the edges.

Cover the bowl with plastic wrap and return to the freezer for at least one hour.

While the ice cream is re-freezing, crush the chocolate graham crackers until crumbly.

Remove the ice cream once again and ensure that it is thoroughly hardened.

Once the ice cream mixture is hardened, use a spatula to spread 2/3 cup of peanut butter over the surface of the ice cream.

Next spread the crushed chocolate graham crackers evenly over the peanut butter.

Return the bowl to the freezer for at least one hour.

Just before an hour is up, fill the sink with warm water.

Remove the bowl from the freezer.

Submerge just the bottom and edges of the bowl in the warm water for about a minute.

The idea is to soften the ice cream around the edges just enough to invert the ice cream onto a plate.

Place a large plate upside down on top of the bowl.

Holding both the bowl and the plate, flip them over together.

Gently tap on the bowl until the ice cream falls to the plate.

Depending on how hard the ice cream has frozen, you may have to return the bowl to the warm water several times.

When the ice cream has safely landed on the plate, cover it with plastic wrap and return to the freezer for another 1-2 hours.

Do not heat fudge topping.

Spread the fudge topping evenly over the surface of the ice cream mountain, like you are frosting a cake.

Refreeze the fudge coated ice cream for an hour.

When the fudge has hardened, frost with the remaining peanut butter.

Again, return to the freezer for at least one hour.

Using a warm knife, slice the ice cream into 12 pieces.

Place wax paper between the cuts for serving convenience.

Return to the freezer covered until ready to serve.

To hear oohs and aahs when you serve the ice cream:

Prepare each plate with a tic-tac-toe pattern of chocolate and caramel sauce.

Create 3 vertical lines of chocolate sauce and three horizontal lines of caramel sauce.

Place the slice of ice cream upright on the plate toward the back of the design.

Top with whipped cream, being quite generous.

Sprinkle with chopped nuts and top with a cherry.

Enjoy before your lovely creation melts.

Repeat for the remaining slices.

Serves 12

Chocolate Peanut Butter Chip Cookies

Ingredients

1 cup sugar
1/2 cup brown sugar
2 sticks (1 cup) butter
2 eggs
2 teaspoons vanilla
1/4 cup Hershey's chocolate syrup
1/2 cup unsweetened cocoa powder
1 cup all-purpose flour
1 cup whole wheat flour
1 teaspoon baking soda
1 1/2 teaspoons kosher salt
1 (12.5-ounce) bag Reese's® peanut butter chips

Instructions

Preheat oven to 375 º F.

Beat together the sugars, shortening, eggs, vanilla, chocolate syrup and cocoa.

Add in the flours, baking soda and salt and combine well.

Lastly stir in the peanut butter chips.

Drop about 2 Tablespoons of the mixture, using either two teaspoons or a cookie scoop, onto the cookie sheet.

Bake for 8 - 9 minutes for one sheet or 10 minutes for two sheets.

The cookies may not look ready but they will be; don't overcook!

Remove from oven and cool on cookie sheet for 5 minutes.

Remove to paper towels or brown paper until completely cool.

Do not use a wire rack as they will harden.

Makes 48 cookies

49

Chocolate Peanut Butter Cream Cheesecake

Ingredients

Crust
9 graham crackers
1/4 cup sugar
½ stick (1/4 cup) melted butter
Cheesecake
3 (8-ounce) packages cream cheese, softened
3 eggs
1 teaspoon vanilla
1 cup sugar
1 1/2 cups semi-sweet chocolate chips, melted
Topping
1/2 cup peanut butter
1/2 cup powdered sugar
1/2 cup heavy cream
1 ounce shaved chocolate

Instructions

Preheat the oven to 350 ° F.

First crush the graham crackers (you can use a food processor).

Blend cracker crumbs, 1/4 cup sugar and melted butter in a small bowl.

Press into base of a 10-inch spring form pan.

Bake for 8 minutes.

Remove from oven and set aside to cool.

In a microwave safe bowl, heat the semi-sweet chocolate until melted and smooth.

Stir at 30 second intervals to avoid scorching.

In a larger mixing bowl, beat cream cheese until smooth.

Mix in sugar and vanilla and blend until smooth.

Add the eggs, one at a time but don't overmix.

Finally add the melted chocolate and combine well.

Pour the mixture over the crust and bake for 45 minutes or until the center is set.

Remove cheesecake from the oven and cool for about 5 minutes.

Remove the outer ring by sliding a knife around the edge.

Allow to cool for 45 minutes.

In a food processor or mixing bowl, mix the peanut butter, cream and powdered sugar until smooth.

Spread over the top of the cooled cheesecake.

Decorate with shaved chocolate.

Refrigerate overnight or for at least 6 hours.

Peanut Butter Chocolate Chip Pound Cake

Ingredients

Cake
3 cups all-purpose flour
1 teaspoon baking powder
1/2 teaspoon salt
1 cup creamy peanut butter (don't use natural)
1/2 cup butter, room temperature
3 cups sugar
6 large eggs
2 teaspoons vanilla
1-1/2 cups chocolate chips

Glaze
1-1/2 cups sifted powdered sugar
1/4 cup milk
1/4 cup creamy peanut butter
1/2 teaspoon vanilla
1/4 cup mini chocolate chips

Instructions

Preheat oven to 325 ° F.

Spray 10-cup tube pan generously with nonstick cooking spray.

Cake

In a medium bowl, stir together flour, baking powder, and salt and set aside.

In a large bowl, using an electric mixer, cream peanut butter and butter.

Add sugar and beat 5 minutes more.

Add eggs and vanilla and beat thoroughly.

Add dry ingredients a little at a time, mixing just until absorbed.

Stir in chopped peanut butter cups.

Pour batter into prepared tube pan, tapping on the counter to remove hidden air pockets.

Bake for 80 minutes (1 hour and 20 minutes) or until a toothpick inserted in center comes out clean.

Check after 1 hour to make sure the cake is not browning too quickly on top.

If it is, place a piece of foil loosely over the top while it continues to cook.

Cool in pan for 20 minutes and then turn onto a rack or platter and let cool completely.

Glaze

In a medium bowl, mix together powdered sugar, milk, peanut butter and vanilla until smooth.

Drizzle glaze over the top and sides of cooled cake.

Sprinkle with a few more chopped peanut butter cups.

The glaze will harden as it cools.

To hasten the glaze's hardening, refrigerate the cake for about 15 minutes.

Makes 12-14 servings

Peanut Butter and Chocolate Biscotti

Ingredients

1 stick plus 2 Tablespoons unsalted butter
2-1/2 cups all-purpose flour
2-3/4 teaspoons baking powder
1/2 teaspoon salt
3 large eggs
1-1/4 cups sugar
2 teaspoons vanilla
1/2 cup smooth natural peanut butter, room temperature
1-1/4 cups dry roasted peanuts
1-1/4 cups chopped dark chocolate or chocolate chunks

Instructions

Position racks evenly apart in the oven.

Preheat oven to 350 ° F.

Line 3 cookie sheets with parchment paper.

In a saucepan over low to medium heat, melt the butter, swirling the pan occasionally.

Continue cooking about 5 minutes, until the butter browns and gives off a nutty aroma.

Cool slightly.

In a large bowl, stir the flour, baking powder, and salt together.

In a medium bowl, using an electric mixer, beat the eggs about 2 minutes, until light and pale yellow.

While continuing to beat, gradually add the sugar.

Slowly add butter and vanilla, mixing about 30 seconds more, until thoroughly combined.

Add the peanut butter and mix thoroughly.

While still mixing slowly, add the dry ingredients in 2 additions, mixing just until absorbed.

Turn off mixer and fold in the peanuts and chocolate pieces.

Evenly divide the dough into thirds, placing each third in the center of a baking sheet.

With your hands slightly wet, shape the dough into logs about 2" wide by 15" long.

Bake 25-30 minutes or until set and brown around the edges.

To ensure even baking, rotate the pans – front to back and top to bottom – about halfway through baking time.

Cool logs on cookie sheets for about 10 minutes.

Lower the oven temperature to 325 º F.

Carefully transfer logs to a cutting board.

Cut logs crosswise diagonally with a long serrated knife, into 1/2-inch thick cookies.

Place cookies cut side down on cookie sheets.

Bake about 8 minutes or until crisp.

Turn cookies over and bake about 8 minutes more or until golden brown.

Cool biscotti on cookie sheets.

Store cookies in an air tight container for up to 3 days.

Mrs. Fields Peanut Butter Dream Bars®

Ingredients

8 Mrs. Fields Chocolate Chip Cookies
5 Tablespoons melted butter
¾ cup peanut butter
1 ½ cups powdered sugar
1 (12-ounce) pkg. milk chocolate chips

Instructions

Preheat oven to 350 ° F.

Crumble the cookies into a medium mixing bowl and add the melted butter.

Stir until the mixture darkens and the butter is thoroughly mixed in.

Firmly press the dough into an ungreased 9 x 9" baking pan.

Bake for 10 minutes or until firm around the edges.

Once the pan has cooled enough to touch, place in the refrigerator.

In another bowl, combine the peanut butter and sugar and blend well.

The mixture should be doughy to allow for kneading by hand.

Microwave the chocolate chips on HIGH for 2 minutes, stirring halfway through the heating time.

When the cookie dough / butter mixture is cool to the touch, remove from refrigerator and spread half of the melted chocolate over the top.

Return to the refrigerator, allowing it to harden for 20-30 minutes more.

Remove from refrigerator and spread the peanut butter mixture evenly over the surface of the chocolate.

Spread the remaining chocolate over the peanut butter, being sure to smooth to the edges of the pan.

Refrigerate until hardened.

Cut into bars.

Makes 10 - 12 bars

Chocolate PBC Ice Cream

Ingredients

Peanut Butter Ice Cream
2-3/4 cups half and half
1 cup regular (not organic or natural) peanut butter
3/4 cup sugar
1/2 teaspoon Kosher salt
1/2 teaspoon vanilla
1 cup chopped peanut butter cups, chilled in freezer

Chocolate Fudge Swirl
1/4 cup light (clear) corn syrup
1/4 cup sugar
2 Tablespoons water
1 Tablespoon canola or vegetable oil
3 ounces unsweetened chocolate
2 Tablespoons Dutch process cocoa powder
1/4 teaspoon Kosher salt

Instructions

Peanut Butter Ice Cream

In a blender, place half and half, peanut butter, sugar, salt, and vanilla.

Blend until smooth.

Transfer to an airtight container and refrigerate for 3 hours or until very cold.

Using an ice cream freezer and following the manufacturer's instructions, free the ice cream.

Transfer ice cream to an airtight container and stir in frozen peanut butter cups.

Chill in freezer.

Chocolate Fudge Swirl

In a heavy saucepan, combine corn syrup, sugar, water, oil, chocolate, cocoa powder, and salt.

On very low heat, cook mixture until chocolate is melted, sugar is fully dissolved, and all ingredients are thoroughly mixed.

Cool the chocolate sauce until it's just warm enough to pour freely from a spoon.

Putting it Together

Remove peanut butter ice cream from the freezer.

Working quickly, fold the fudge sauce into ice cream with a large spoon or rubber spatula.

Fold in—don't stir—the sauce just until swirl is distributed.

Immediately return to the freezer and chill at least 3 hours or until firm.

Chocolate Peanut Butter Cake

Ingredients

Cake
1 box devil's food cake mix
1 small package instant chocolate pudding mix
1 cup sour cream
1 cup vegetable oil
4 eggs, beaten
1/2 cup milk
1 teaspoon vanilla
2 cups quartered miniature peanut butter cups

Peanut Butter Frosting
2 sticks (1 cup) butter
4 cups powdered sugar
1/4 teaspoon salt
1 teaspoon vanilla extract
1/3 cup heavy whipping cream
½ cup smooth peanut butter

Instructions

Cake

Preheat oven to 350 ° F.

In a large mixing bowl, mix all the ingredients except for the quartered peanut butter cups.

The mixture should have a nice, thick consistency.

Stir in peanut butter cups.

Pour the mixture into two 9-inch pie pans.

Bake for approximately 45 minutes until done.

(Use the time on the cake mix box plus 10 minutes as a guide. Check it regularly as it bakes).

Frosting

In a mixing bowl, cream the butter until light and fluffy.
Add the sugar and continue to cream until well blended.
Add salt, vanilla and whipping cream.
Blend on a low speed until combined well.
Beat at high speed until fluffy.

Chocolate Peanut Butter Cream Pie

Ingredients

¾ cup hot fudge ice cream topping, divided
1 (6-ounce) Graham cracker Crust
½ cup creamy peanut butter
1-1/4 cups cold milk
2 (3.4-ounce) packages Vanilla Instant Pudding
8 ounces Cool Whip, thawed, divided

Instructions

Spread 1/2 cup fudge topping into crust and freeze for 10 minutes.

In large bowl, combine peanut butter and milk until well blended.

Add both dry pudding mixes and beat for 2 minutes. This will be thick.

Add half the Cool Whip and mix thoroughly.

Pour into crust and top with remaining Cool Whip.

Chill in refrigerator for 3 hours or until firm.

Just before serving, drizzle with remaining fudge topping.

63

Chocolate Peanut Butter Bark

Ingredients

2 pounds (32 ounces) semisweet chocolate chips
1-½ cups creamy peanut butter
About 1 cup mini pretzels, broken into smaller pieces, more or less to cover a layer
2 cups powdered sugar
6 Tablespoons unsalted butter, melted
1 teaspoon vanilla

Instructions

Melt half the chocolate chips in a microwave for about 30 seconds.

Spread evenly over parchment paper or a paper-lined cookie sheet.

Create a large rectangle, approximately ⅛″ to ¼″ thick.

Place in the freezer to set.

In a large bowl, combine peanut butter, powdered sugar, melted butter and vanilla until smooth and creamy.

Remove chocolate layer from the freezer.

Spread peanut butter mixture over the top.

Sprinkle with pretzel pieces and press into the peanut butter.

Return the bark to the freezer to harden again.

Melt the remaining chocolate chips.

Remove the bark from the freezer and top with the remainder of the chocolate.

Chill or freeze until set.

Break the bark into small pieces using a butcher knife or ice pick.

Keep cool in the refrigerator or freezer until ready to serve.

Printed in Great Britain
by Amazon.co.uk, Ltd.,
Marston Gate.